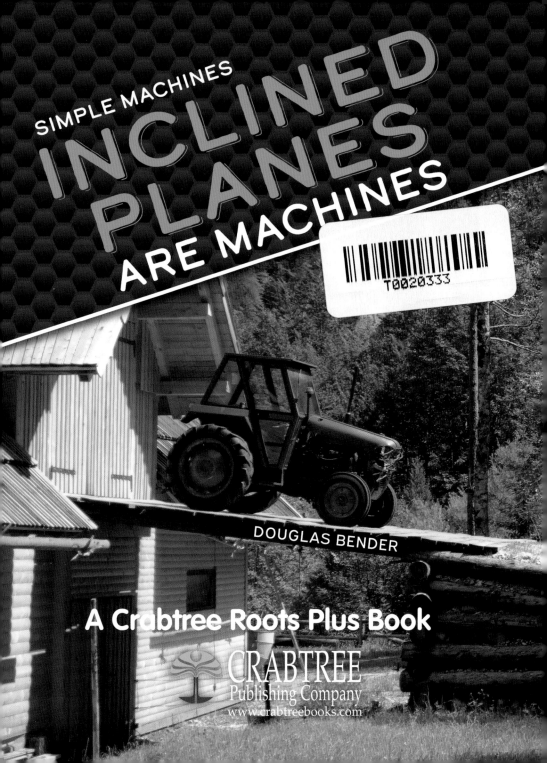

SIMPLE MACHINES

INCLINED PLANES

ARE MACHINES

T0020333

DOUGLAS BENDER

A Crabtree Roots Plus Book

CRABTREE
Publishing Company
www.crabtreebooks.com

School-to-Home Support for Caregivers and Teachers

This book helps children grow by letting them practice reading. Here are a few guiding questions to help the reader with building his or her comprehension skills. Possible answers appear here in red.

Before Reading:

- What do I think this book is about?
    - *I think this book is about inclined planes.*
    - *I think this book is about how inclined planes help us in our everyday life.*
- What do I want to learn about this topic?
    - *I want to learn about real-world examples of inclined planes.*
    - *I want to learn about what makes an inclined plane a simple machine.*

During Reading:

- I wonder why...
    - *I wonder why a staircase is an inclined plane.*
    - *I wonder why inclined planes are different sizes.*
- What have I learned so far?
    - *I have learned that a slide at the park is an inclined plane.*
    - *I have learned that some roads are inclined planes.*

After Reading:

- What details did I learn about this topic?
    - *I have learned that people who depend on wheelchairs use inclined planes.*
    - *I have learned that simple machines have few or no moving parts.*
- Read the book again and look for the vocabulary words.
    - *I see the word **stairs** on page 10 and the word **slide** on page 20. The other vocabulary words are found on page 23.*

This is an **inclined plane**.

Pulley

Lever

Screw

It is one of six **simple machines**.

Wedge

Inclined Plane

Wheel and Axle

Simple machines have few or no moving parts.

Inclined planes help us lift and lower things.

Some inclined planes are long.

The inclined planes on this road help cars move up the mountain.

Jordan runs up the **stairs**.

He is using an inclined plane!

People who use **wheelchairs** depend on inclined planes.

Some inclined planes are short.

This **moving truck** has a short inclined plane.

The back of this truck
is an inclined plane.

It makes dumping
the **load** easier.

Inclined planes can also be fun!

A **slide** is a fun inclined plane.

Word List

Sight Words

a	moving	up
also	no	us
and	or	use
are	parts	using
few	people	who
have	runs	
he	some	
help	the	
is	things	
long	this	

Words to Know

inclined plane

load

moving truck

simple machines

slide

stairs

wheelchairs

Written by: Douglas Bender
Designed by: Rhea Wallace
Series Development: James Earley
Proofreader: Janine Deschenes
Production coordinator
    and Prepress technician: Katherine Berti
Print coordinator: Katherine Berti
Educational Consultant: Marie Lemke M.Ed.

Photographs:
Shutterstock: Andrej Safaric: cover, p. 1; Dushlik: p.3, 23; Ryan Fletcher: p. 7; Flystock: p. 8-9; Natchar Lai: p. 11; XArt Production: p. 13; 24-K Production: p. 14; Christina Richards: p. 15, 23; David Pruter: p. 16-17, 23; Juris Vigulis: p. 19; Iakov Filimanor:p. 21, 23

SIMPLE MACHINES
INCLINED PLANES
ARE MACHINES

Library and Archives Canada
Cataloguing in Publication

CIP available at Library and Archives Canada

Library of Congress
Cataloging-in-Publication Data

CIP available at Library of Congress

Crabtree Publishing Company

www.crabtreebooks.com   1-800-387-7650

Printed in the U.S.A./CG20210915/012022

Published in the United States
Crabtree Publishing
347 Fifth Avenue, Suite 1402-145
New York, NY, 10016

Published in Canada
Crabtree Publishing
616 Welland Ave.
St. Catharines, ON, L2M 5V6